Cricket
RULES

Cricket
RULES

TOM SHEPHERD

BLANDFORD

A BLANDFORD BOOK

First published in the UK by Blandford
An imprint of Cassell plc
Cassell plc, Wellington House, 125 Strand,
London WC2R 0BB

Distributed in Australia by Capricorn Link
(Australia) Pty Ltd
2/13 Carrington Road, Castle Hill, NSW 2154

British Library Cataloguing-in-Publication Data
A catalogue entry for this title is available from
the British Library

ISBN 0-7137-2509-5

Typeset by Litho Link Ltd, Welshpool, Powys,
Wales

Printed and bound in the U.K. by
The Bath Press, Avon

Frontispiece Stumped! The bails are off
before Robin Smith has regained his ground.

CONTENTS

INTRODUCTION

There is a danger in producing a summarized version of a set of the rules of cricket; you run the risk of omitting the very details which the reader seeks. The aim in this book, however, is to explain cricket in a style relevant to the needs of the average follower of the game. Cricket boasts a vast literature – often dry and legalistic and only suitable for the expert.

The Laws of cricket – first set by the Marylebone Cricket Club (MCC) and, now, maintained and revised in collaboration with the Test and County Cricket Board (TCCB) and other international bodies – are not only complex but also relate to a more complicated contest, the professional game. Amateur cricket coaches, players, and administrators outnumber professionals by many thousands. They do not need laws which are only applicable to games of more than one innings, often played over several days, for monetary reward and on grounds which boast sophisticated preparation

and maintenance equipment.

This volume is therefore aimed at the schoolteacher, parent, amateur coach or player who has to learn for himself, or to pass on to others, the essential legislation which controls the game. Increasingly, many schools are no longer devoting fully trained coaches to outdoor sports. Others may not have the facilities to play competitive cricket. The result is that clubs and parents are called upon to teach the game.

This book will not make extensive reference to the rules and interpretations which are the sole preserve of the professional game, where the smallest matter of law can affect a career, a league position or financial earnings. It will also ignore the laws set up exclusively for particular professional competitions; these are created for those tournaments only and are not part of the official rules of cricket.

The comments above should not be

taken as a disregard for the MCC rule book. On the contrary, this book has at its heart the belief that the legislation of the game has played, and must continue to play, a fundamental role in cricket. Only by strict adherence to the official Laws, which have stood the test of time, will the game be able to resist plans for wholesale revision while retaining its traditional virtues of fairness and correctness. Particular rules and their value can be debated at length, and should be, to ensure a healthy awareness of the needs of a sport in a changing world; but such discussions have no place on the pitch. For readers who wish to have a copy of the full version of the official Laws of cricket, it is best to apply directly to the MCC at Lord's Cricket Ground in London.

Around the world new nations and fresh generations are turning to cricket as a team game in which the individual can shine but where the full squad has a role to play. To ensure cricket's prosperity this expansion must take place against a background of respect for and knowledge of its laws and a readiness to preserve its reputation for sportsmanship and good etiquette.

● AUTHOR'S NOTE

For the sake of convenience and ease of reading, male terms are used throughout the book. Explaining this enables the author to make reference to the giant strides being taken by women's cricket around the world; long may it continue.

THE GROUND AND THE PITCH

One of the enduring delights of cricket and a reason for its popularity is that you can learn the game with just a bat and ball and some measure of open space. Cricket has always been played informally – on beaches, in back yards, and at the perimeter of formal games where few youngsters can watch a match for long without wanting to start up one of their own; we will all have seen a bottle or stick and a tightly rolled ball of paper being used with a fence or a back-street lamp-post providing the wicket.

The rules of cricket in respect of the ground on which it is played are written with the professional game in mind but it is as well to acknowledge some basic fundamentals which should be employed at all permanent cricket grounds where competitive matches are likely to be played. These need not necessarily be extensive grounds with luxurious amenities, but any venue should meet certain standards.

● THE BOUNDARY

The **boundary** of the playing area has to be established before the game begins. Where a permanent object, such as a wall, exists then that may well be taken as the boundary though, for safety's sake, it would be better for a line to be created a yard or two inside it. On open ground, a white line or a series of markers should be used to define the boundary; a combination of the two is ideal and avoids dispute. The best boundary of all is a rope.

Fixed items at any position within the boundary line – the most common are trees and the sightscreens – will normally also be regarded as a boundary mark. Thus, if a rolling or bouncing ball hits a tree or passes underneath a sightscreen before it reaches the boundary it will be signalled as a 'four' and if it hits the object on the full, a 'six' will normally

Boundary marker

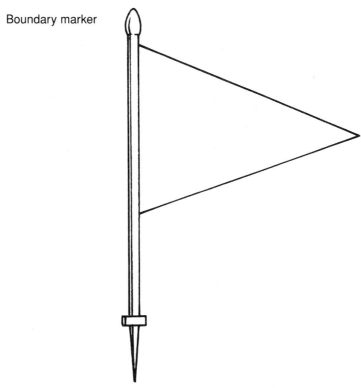

The ideal boundary marking – a rope with
intermittent flags.

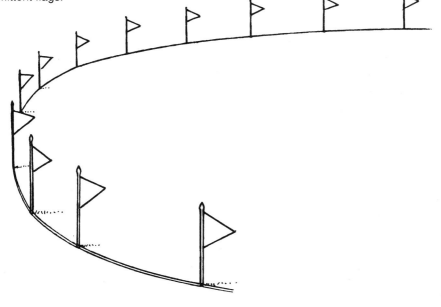

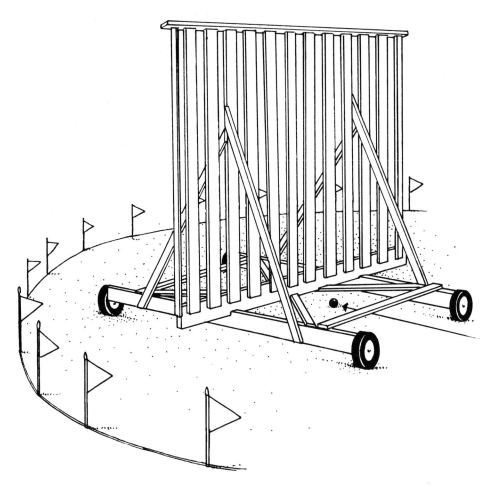

be given, even if it is clear that the ball would otherwise have fallen within the perimeter markings. (Methods of scoring are explained in the chapter on 'Scoring and Scorers'.)

Many grounds have trees which overhang the boundary. If a lofted shot strikes these branches but still falls within the line it will normally be called a 'six' and should that ball be 'caught' by a fielder the batsman will be given 'not out'. Local rules may be applied where the ground is small or

A sightscreen within the boundary. A ball rolling to the position shown will be signalled a boundary four.

one boundary especially short. While it is the job of the visiting captain and umpires to establish such matters before the toss, it is courteous of the host captain to provide the information before being asked.

Size of the ground
Except for the top amateur leagues

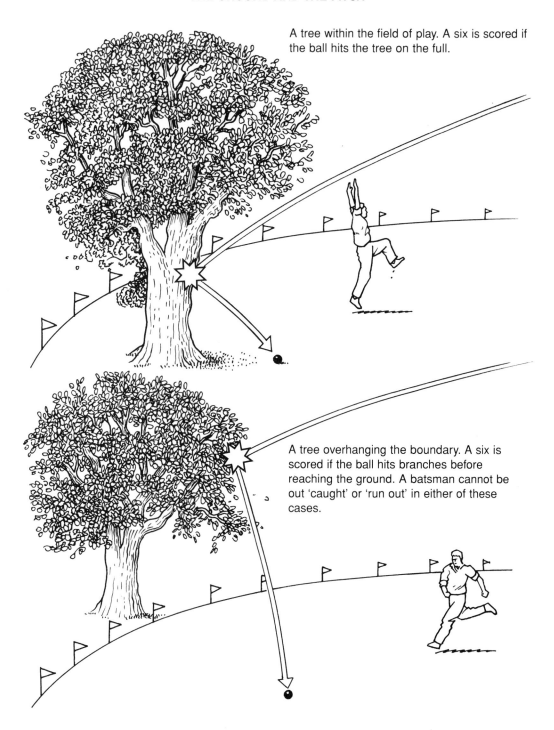

A tree within the field of play. A six is scored if the ball hits the tree on the full.

A tree overhanging the boundary. A six is scored if the ball hits branches before reaching the ground. A batsman cannot be out 'caught' or 'run out' in either of these cases.

and the professional game there is no rule stipulating the size of the area used for cricket. Where a large area is available for colts or junior cricket it is advisable to shorten the boundaries by using temporary markers.

● PREPARATION OF THE GROUND

Here again no rules apply at local or schools cricket level and if the ground is being hired from, and therefore maintained by, a third party like a council or a club, influence over its preparation may be limited. The joy of cricket is increased if it is played on a freshly cut and well-tended area of good grass; organizers of youth cricket should endeavour to play on the best outfield possible as young players can be injured by falling on bare or rough surfaces or by misfielding a ball bouncing over uneven ground.

The pitch
The most important item of 'equipment' in cricket is the surface the game is played on. A well-prepared, flat **pitch** will be safe for the batsmen and will produce a good game. Because of the widely differing climates around the world of cricket, and the growth of the use of artificial wickets for junior and social cricket, there are no laws regarding the nature and appearance of pitches. But the measurements *are* set (Law 7/8) and are as follows:

	Adult	Junior*
Length of the pitch	22 yd (20.12 m)	21 yd (19.20 m)
Height of stumps	28 in (71.1 cm)	27 in (68.58 cm)
Width of stumps	9 in (22.86 cm)	8 in (20.32 cm)
Bail width	4.75 in (12.1 cm)	3.87 in (9.84 cm)

*The measurements may change for younger colts and be set by local League administrators.

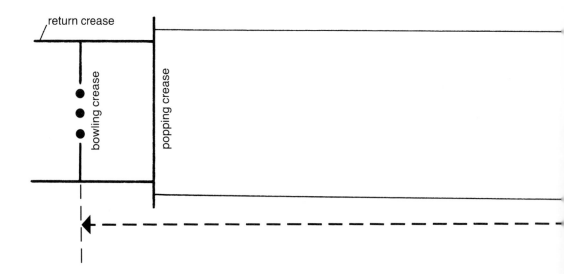

Above A sightscreen within the field of play.   *Below* The measurements of a cricket pitch for a senior game.

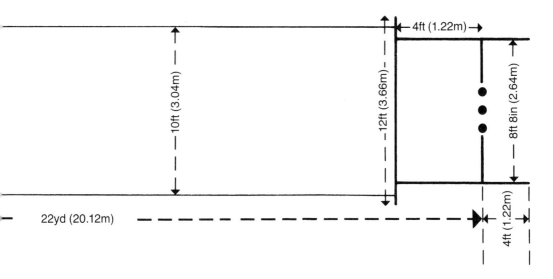

Stumps and bails are made to these standard dimensions and to various qualities; bails can be purchased in heavier wood to prevent them from being accidentally dislodged in high winds. Such bails should only be

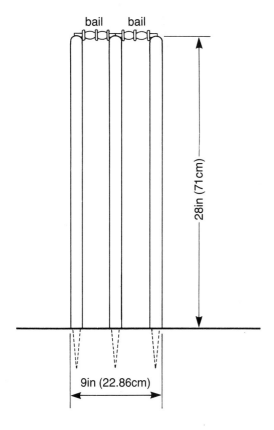

The wicket

employed with the consent of both teams.

The width of the pitch is deemed to be 10ft but may not always be cut to this measure by the groundsman; the width of the **bowling crease** (Law 9) is 8ft 8in (2.64m) though the front (**popping crease**) line should be a minimum of 12ft (3.66m) and there is no limit to its length across the field. These **creases** are linked by side lines of 4ft (1.22m) which extend by the same distance again behind the bowling crease to form the **return crease** (see diagram). The stumps are set in the centre of the bowling crease.

The most important element of the rules as they affect the crease marking is that the thickness of the line is unimportant as, for a batsman making or staying in his ground, some part of his bat in his hand, or his person, must be grounded *behind the line*. On the line is *out*. For a bowler in his delivery stride, his feet must be *behind*, or *within*, the relevant lines. Thus, the back or inside edge of any line is what is critical, not its width.

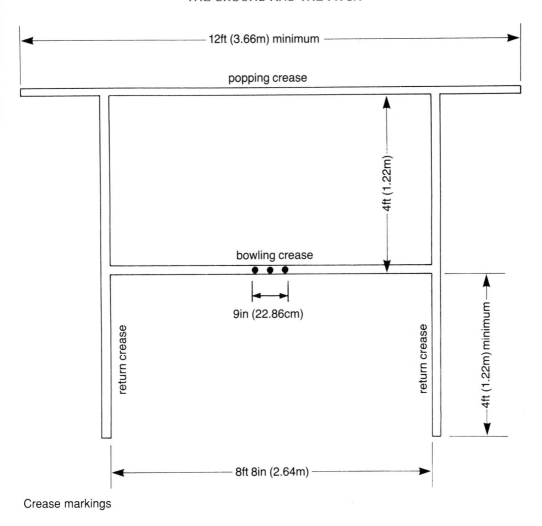

Crease markings

Overleaf Trees overhanging the boundary. If the ball strikes the branches on the fall a boundary six will be signalled even if the ball lands inside the boundary markers.

● CONDITION OF THE GROUND AND PITCH

There are no rules about the state of the pitch, except for those under Law 3.8. This states that the preparation of the ground will be in the hands of the host club or the ground authority and players and umpires will have limited responsibility or influence over its being made ready for the game. The umpires should inspect the pitch prior to the match (see the chapter on 'Umpires' below) but only after the toss has been made can they assume any involvement or judgement as to its fitness or otherwise. Should its condition alter during play, through the effect of bad weather or other factors, the umpires are the sole arbiters of its fitness and only they can raise the issue of suspending or abandoning the match.

The mower and roller are the primary items of equipment in pitch maintenance and most surfaces will perform badly if they are not rolled frequently. Once the game commences the pitch can only be rolled between innings at the request of the team batting next (Law 10). If the start of the match is delayed the batting side's captain may ask for a rolling though the umpires may overrule this if they believe the consequent delay outweighs the value of the work.

It is not always possible to assess the quality of a pitch before play and even its early behaviour can be misleading. The umpires have the right to delay or abandon the game if they consider the pitch to be unfit and, in such circumstances, are also empowered to allow a change of pitch in order for a game to continue.

Though covers are not common below professional and top amateur levels, two simple heavy-duty plastic sheets measuring 15 ft × 12 ft or longer can be used to protect the ends of the pitch (Law 11.3) prior to a match when further rainfall could prejudice the start. However, the pitch cannot be fully covered during a match (Law 11.2). The repair of a pitch during a game is restricted to such work as can be undertaken by the use of a bat or sawdust, provided the ground is not damaged by this action. For games of more than one day, bowlers' footholes may, with the umpire's agreement, be filled or returfed. It is useful to good umpiring and player safety as well as courteous if the crease markings are brushed and re-marked between innings.

Artificial pitches

These are increasingly used by schools and for social cricket. The rules state (Law 7.4) that the pitch should measure 58 ft (17.68 m) by 6 ft (1.83 m). Owners of such pitches should appreciate that a poorly maintained covering can soon fall short of these measures if grass is allowed to grow over the edges.

THE TEAMS

● THE PLAYERS

The rules (Law 1) call for there to be eleven players in each team, one of whom should be nominated as captain with a further player chosen as a deputy.

It is not common in the amateur game for captains to exchange team sheets but it is nevertheless sensible to ensure that all parties are aware of expected latecomers – should any specific rules under which the game is being played not forbid latecomers from taking part.

The captain
The player selected as captain is responsible (Law 42) for ensuring that play is conducted within the spirit of the game as well as according to the rules. This can be considered a vague stipulation unless the selected player understands that it does, in truth, charge him to control the attitude and demeanour of his team and to uphold the traditional sporting values and etiquette of cricket.

Leaving the field
A player may not leave the field without the agreement of the umpire at the bowler's end. (For the rules on substitution see the chapter on 'Fielding' on p. 74.) If a member of the fielding side leaves the pitch, or fails to return after an interval, for more than 15 minutes, he is not allowed to bowl after his return until he has been back on the field for the same time he was absent.

THE BAT AND THE BALL

● THE CRICKET BAT

The dimensions of the cricket bat, but not its weight, are controlled (Law 6).

The bat – from the 'toe' of the blade to the top of the handle – must not measure more than 38 in (96.5 cm) and the blade not be more than 4.25 in (10.8 cm) at its widest part. The blade has to be made of wood but can be covered by additional material to protect the face or repair damage provided that this does not exceed $\frac{1}{16}$ in (1.56 mm) in thickness.

There seems no end to the refinements to the traditional shape of the cricket bat that manufacturers can come up with – usually with the aim of creating 'this year's model' which players of all ages want to be seen with. Some changes are pure gimmickry, others claim to give an easier 'pick up', or a larger 'sweet spot';

there are, of course, bats at various prices and those which are more expensive can be expected to use a better quality of willow (all bats are made from this wood). To stay within a sensible weight – most adult players find it difficult to play well with a bat weighing more than 3 lb – batmakers have taken to cutting grooves in order to leave more wood at the edges, centre or toe. Other innovations have seen bats with two 'faces' and another with a crooked handle!

As all reputable makers conform to the measurements laid down in the Laws there are very few instances of contravention but, with the bat so much a part of the game, administrators at all levels have to remain watchful for examples of tampering.

Smaller bats are made for juniors. For the serious younger player it is important that his bat is right for his size (i.e. not too large) throughout his growing years.

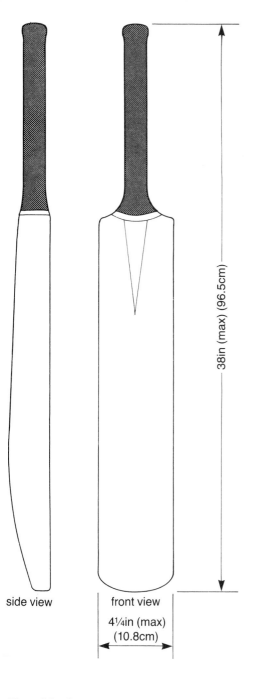

side view   front view

38in (max) (96.5cm)

4¼in (max)
(10.8cm)

The cricket bat

● THE CRICKET BALL

A new cricket ball must conform to official rules (Law 5). A top grade ball should not weigh less than 5½oz (155.9g) nor more than 5¾oz (163g) and not measure less than 8¹³⁄₁₆in (22.4cm) nor more than 9in (22.9cm) in circumference. There are measurements and weight ranges within which other balls must fall; they are:

> Men's: (Lesser grade balls) 5⁵⁄₁₆oz (150g) to 5¹³⁄₁₆oz (165g)
> 8¹¹⁄₁₆in (22cm) to 9¹⁄₁₆in (23cm)
> Women's: 4¹⁵⁄₁₆oz (140g) to 5⁵⁄₁₆oz (150g)
> 8¼in (21cm) to 8⅞in (22.5cm)
> Junior: 4⁵⁄₁₆oz (133g) to 5¹⁄₁₆oz (143g)
> 8¹⁄₁₆in (20.5cm) to 8¹¹⁄₁₆in (22cm)

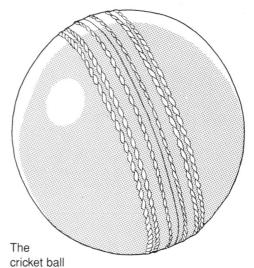

The cricket ball

Balls manufactured by established companies can be expected to meet these specifications but with the ball being, along with the bat and the playing surface, one of the basic elements of the sport, club officials and umpires should guard against sub-standard examples being used. Where one ball is used for an entire game the team using it for the second part of the match can be at a grave disadvantage if its quality has deteriorated. Where a new ball is provided for each innings it is important that they have identical properties and playing characteristics. Though the cost of cricket equipment is considerable, savings should not be made when purchasing balls and careful watch should be kept on makes and designs which perform well and provide good value for money.

Balls of all standards are liable to have occasional faults. If a deterioration, other than normal wear and tear, is brought to the umpires' attention they can consider changing it for one of equal quality and condition. Umpires should, however, guard against over-zealous complaints from a fielding side, as a new ball will generally benefit them.

When a ball is replaced during an innings both batsmen and the captain of the fielding side must be advised. However, the decision as to whether a ball should be changed rests entirely with the umpires.

THE UMPIRES

It is probably only after you have played in a match controlled by well-qualified umpires that you truly appreciate their value. For all the criticism they may attract – and even the top international officials get their share – the game will suffer if it is in the hands of people who do not know or have little respect for the rules and traditions of the game. A good cricket match is always monitored by wise and experienced officials.

Most cricket around the world is not umpired by formally qualified or professional personnel; it is more likely to be overseen by teachers, parents, players or supporters who, often under duress, agree to 'stand'. However, even if the official is not thoroughly versed in every nuance of the rule book it is imperative that all 22 players abide by his decision, without debate, even if their knowledge of the laws is more thorough than the umpire's.

There will never be enough umpires.

Most team games struggle to find enough volunteers, especially at amateur and social levels. Since every player should have a working knowledge of cricket's Laws it should be a short step from there to undertaking umpiring duties if and when required. Even though it may not be the case for everyone, many players will find umpiring adds interest to their game if they occasionally view it impartially from close quarters. Certainly all young players should be encouraged to learn the 'how to' element of umpiring as this will give them the confidence to take on the role at a later date and instil in them the need to control a game effectively.

It may not be necessary for occasional umpires to apply themselves as completely to the work as this chapter suggests but, to use the popular adage, if a job is worth doing, it is worth doing well. Taking the job seriously will make you a better umpire and may even encourage you to take one of the many courses held by the various county and regional associations around the world.

● PREPARATION

How the umpire looks and is equipped may not be part of the Laws of cricket but it is worth setting the highest standards in this most important role.

To start as you mean to go on, kit yourself out properly even if the umpire's coat you are supplied with may have seen better days. If you umpire regularly you will want to have your own coat to suit your own particular needs.

The checklist of essential equipment:

Counters Pebbles or coins are the favourites but convenient counting 'machines' are manufactured and some umpires invent their own means of counting, e.g. washers on a small rod.

Watch Both umpires should wear a watch and the two watches should be synchronized. If the timing of a match is monitored according to a clock at the ground, the umpires should match their watches to that.

Pen and paper You may need to keep a record of overs bowled and bowlers used – if the match requires this a card may be provided but, in any event,

various styles are manufactured. An umpire may also need to record incidents or get a written message to the scorers. On wet days, care should be taken to keep everything dry.

Balls The umpire should take the field with the ball provided for the start of the game. He should also carry at least one used ball in good condition to replace damaged match balls and be aware of where a further supply can be reached at short notice. Most importantly, the umpire should ensure that the ball is returned to him at any break in play.

Bails These will be provided by the host club. A regular umpire may choose to carry his own set.

Bowler's marker These may well be supplied by the host club but the efficient umpire will carry his own. Whichever markers are used the diligent umpire will recover them at the end of the match to ensure no damage is caused to mowing machinery.

Drying cloths Even on dry days there can be the need to clean a ball so each umpire should have a cloth to dry or clean the ball.

The Laws of Cricket An umpire may choose to carry this book or a copy of the MCC Laws of Cricket, or a book of local rules. Where League or other rules apply to a game, both umpires should also carry a copy of these or ensure one is kept by the scorers.

● DRESS

The famous white coat has been significantly altered in recent years to provide extra loops, pockets and other features of value to the modern umpire. In warm weather it is now accepted practice to discard the coat and work in a white shirt. Whatever the conditions, the umpire should be suitably kitted out so that he is comfortable and able to concentrate fully on his job. The smart official engenders respect and portrays confidence.

● DUTIES

The umpire who takes his job seriously has plenty to do before the game. He does not need to undertake this work in an overly officious way and, if he is umpiring at a ground he knows, not all the following checks will be required.

Well before the scheduled start he should, ideally with his fellow umpire:

A smartly dressed umpire giving clear signals and decisions presents a figure of authority.

- meet with any groundsman available
- inspect the ground conditions and the wicket. (In the event of any condition being found which might prejudice the start of the match or the players' safety, the umpire should request it to be attended to. This could include a damaged outfield, an unsafe water tap cover, obstacles on the field of play, etc.)
- check what materials are provided to counter wet weather, e.g. covers, sawdust, etc.
- meet with the captains and scorers; ascertain the position the latter will take up for the match
- obtain the match ball, used balls and bails
- check the toss takes place in good time and note the result
- take the field with his fellow umpire at least five minutes prior to the scheduled start
- check the alignment of the stumps and place the bails.

The umpire from whose end the first over is to be bowled should then:

- check that the scorers are in position and ready
- ascertain the bowler's action (left or right arm, over or around the wicket) and advise the batsman taking the first ball
- assist the batsman in taking a guard and in the adjustment of the position of any sightscreen
- ensure the fielding side have no more than eleven players on the field

- hand the ball to the bowler or his captain
- check that the batsman and other umpire are ready
- check that the agreed starting time has been reached and call 'Play.'

During the match the umpires should work as a team. Whether they have been independently appointed or are representatives of the clubs involved each man should assist the other by keeping count of the balls bowled, even when standing at the striker's end, being alert enough to give the decisions which are his to give (such as run outs and stumpings) and advise on other factors where he may be better positioned than his colleague, such as the fairness of a catch or a ball reaching the boundary.

A typical checklist of duties for the umpire at the bowler's end would be:

- count the number of balls, allowing for no-balls to be added, and call 'Over' at the completion of the set number
- signal all boundaries, 'byes' and 'leg byes'; call and signal 'wides'; 'no-balls' as relevant to his location and 'short runs' at his end; call and signal 'dead ball' as required
- answer appeals for bowled, leg before wicket, handled the ball, hit the ball twice, obstruction, timed out, and run out at his end
- announce the termination of play at intervals and at the end of the match, and signal when the last hour of play commences
- watch for all instances of unfair play

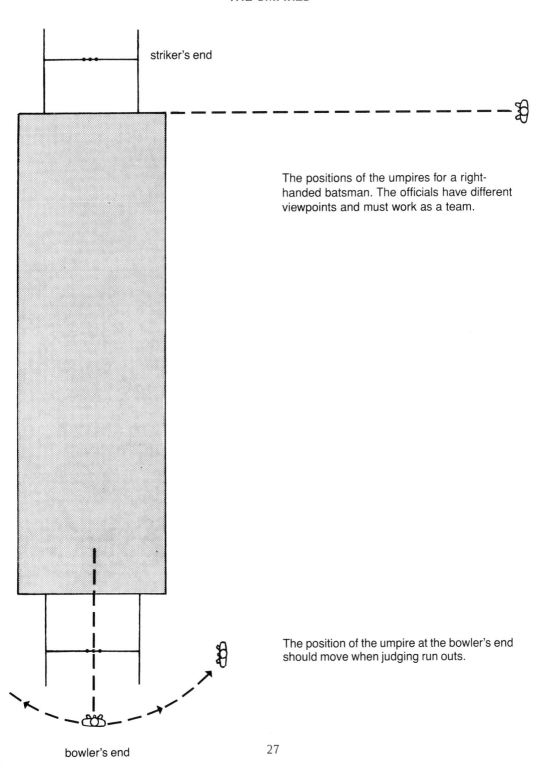

striker's end

The positions of the umpires for a right-handed batsman. The officials have different viewpoints and must work as a team.

The position of the umpire at the bowler's end should move when judging run outs.

bowler's end

and pitch damage and act when necessary

- administer the law in respect of players leaving the field
- check that his signals are acknowledged by the scorers and that the scores are being displayed correctly.

The umpire at the striker's end must not be idle for his duties include:

- count the number of balls bowled as a back-up for his colleague
- signal 'short runs' at his end, 'no-balls' in respect of the bowler's action or the leg-side field, and 'dead ball' where applicable
- answer appeals for 'hit wicket', 'stumped', and 'run out' at his end
- watch for the position of batsmen when runs are being attempted so as to adjudicate on queries as to whether the batsmen have 'crossed'
- watch for all instances of unfair play and act when necessary
- check that the scores are being displayed correctly.

The umpires should act together during intervals to identify the batsmen and bowlers in action at the cessation of play, record the remaining number of balls to be bowled if play ceased before an over was completed, supervise any work undertaken on the pitch and ensure the set time for the interval is kept to. It is clear that the umpires' jobs are far from the obvious adjudication of appeals; good umpires will often be taken for granted if doing their job well.

● UMPIRING SIGNALS

The drawings on pp. 30–1 illustrate the correct signals made by umpires to players and scorers. They should be made clearly, without gimmick and at the right moment. Where calls are made alongside a visual signal, these should be strong, clear and timely.

● DEFINITION OF A BROKEN WICKET

Either bail must be fully dislodged for the wicket to be broken. This can be done by a fieldsman's hand or arm provided the ball is under control in that hand. If the wicket is broken by an unsuccessful dismissal or accident it can be rebuilt by a member of the fielding side while the ball is still in play. If the wicket is already broken when a further run out or stumping is attempted then the player must remove a standing stump from the ground with the ball under control in his hands. If all the stumps are out of the ground the fielding side must replace one in order to break the wicket.

If bails are permanently removed because of high wind, it is up to the umpires to judge whether the stumps have been hit and wicket broken.

● UNFAIR PLAY

Examples of unfair play not referred to elsewhere in this book include the following:

Obstruction of a batsman running
A member of the fielding side who deliberately hinders the batsmen running between the wickets will be warned by the umpire. In such circumstances the umpire will call 'Dead Ball' and allow completed runs, any run in progress or any boundary scored.

Time wasting
At the first example of wilful time wasting the umpire will warn the captain of the team concerned. If such unfair play is repeated the umpire may choose to report the incidents to the officials of the club and the organizers of the competition under whose rules the game has been played.

Players damaging the pitch
Wilful damage to the playing surface can be caused by a bowler repeatedly running onto the danger area (see the chapter on bowling), fielders deliberately causing wear to this section of the pitch or the batsman using undue force or frequency with his bat in his supposed repair of the playing surface. In all instances the umpire will employ the same warning pattern.

Stealing runs
It is considered unfair play if the batsmen attempt a run while the bowler is walking back to his mark or during his run to the wicket unless he first attempts a run out (Law 24).

Umpiring signals

No Ball

Out

Boundary 6

Bye

Boundary 4

Wide

Short Run

Dead Ball

Leg Bye

STARTING THE GAME

The Laws of cricket specify only that the start of each innings and the recommencement of play after an interval for refreshment or other reasons should be signalled by the umpire at the bowler's end calling 'Play', that no practice may take place on the pitch on the day of the game and that bowlers shall not be allowed a trial run-up after the game has started except at a pause in play such as the loss of a wicket when the umpire may allow such practice if it will not delay the game.

Though the starting time is not covered in the official rules, most matches have an official start time and league matches may be governed by hours of play set out in the rules of that competition. It is the umpires' responsibility to see that the field is ready for play well in advance of the set starting time. The captains should ensure that the toss is conducted early enough for the match to start on time.

● INTERVALS IN PLAY

If the match is not governed by League or Competition rules which set the timing and duration of intervals, the captains must make sure they and the umpires are agreed on when these breaks will occur. This should include drinks breaks, if relevant, for considerable advantages can be obtained by such a pause in the match being wrongly timed or unduly extended.

Graeme Hick ducks under a bouncer.

SCORING AND THE SCORERS

● SCORING RUNS

Runs are the basic scoring unit in cricket. They can be scored by three means:

- by the batsmen running from crease to crease and making their ground while the ball is in play; this applies whether the batsman has hit the ball or not
- by the ball reaching or crossing the perimeter of the playing area
- by the umpires awarding penalty runs.

A run can be attempted after the ball is hit, or runs for byes, leg byes (provided the striker has tried to hit the ball) or wides. Provided neither batsman is caught, run out, or otherwise dismissed, the runs completed are added to the total score. If a fielder throws the ball past his teammates guarding the stumps (**overthrows**) further runs can be attempted; a boundary is scored if the misdirected throw reaches or passes over the boundary. All runs scored as overthrows are credited to the batsman on strike for the ball concerned if the ball has been hit, or to the total of **extras** if the initial run is made for byes, leg byes or wides. If the batsmen cross for one run but the overthrow goes for a boundary four then the total runs scored will be five and the batsman initially on strike will remain at the non-striker's end he had run to for the single run.

Four runs or more can be scored by means other than boundaries and overthrows. A fast-running batting pair can complete an all-run four (or more) while the ball runs to an unguarded sector of the outfield. In the unlikely event that they run more than four before the ball reaches the boundary the striker is credited with the runs completed, but not the boundary score.

The nature and positioning of the

A fielder may lean against a low board or fence when stopping or catching the ball but must not step on or over a rope or line.

boundary markings will be established by the umpires before play (see the chapter on 'Umpires') and, excepting where local rules apply, boundaries are scored when the ball touches or crosses the boundary line while in play or a fielder in possession of the ball touches or grounds any part of his body on or behind the marker or over a boundary fence or board. It should be noted here that a fielder may legally lean against a low fence or board to prevent a boundary or attempt a catch; in this respect, there is a distinction between a boundary mark indicated by a painted line, rope or intermittent markers, and a low, permanent board, wall or fence.

If a rolling ball is stopped by a fielder within the field of play but his motion carries him beyond the boundary while in possession of the ball then a boundary four is awarded. If he catches the ball on the full but carries the ball out of play it is not a fair catch, the batsman is not given out and a six will be signalled.

If a ball runs under or strikes a sightscreen which is wholly or partly within the field of play a boundary four is scored. If such a hit travels over the screen a six will be given even if the ball still falls within the boundary markings. Remember, though, that local customs may override these rules.

Penalty runs are scored when no-balls and wides are bowled, when a fielder stops the ball illegally or the ball strikes an object, such as a helmet, discarded by a fielder, and when a ball is lost within the field of play. For fielding penalties, for example, when the ball strikes a discarded helmet, five runs are awarded, in addition to any runs completed before the incident. If the batsman strikes the ball the resulting penalty runs are added to his score; otherwise they count as extras. If a fielder chooses to call 'Lost Ball' then six runs are added to the score but if more than six runs have been completed when the call is made then this number shall count.

● LOSING RUNS

Runs are lost or sacrificed in the following circumstances:

- by an umpire calling 'One Short' on seeing a batsman fail to make his ground before attempting a further run
- when a batsman is caught out he sacrifices any run completed while the ball was in the air
- when a batsman is run out, the run he is attempting is not counted
- when a batsman obstructs a fielder making a catch none of the runs attempted are allowed.

A batsman only 'makes his ground' when the bat in his hand or part of his body touches the ground *behind* the

popping crease; efficient umpires will watch for players failing to do this when turning for a further run. If both batsmen run short only a single can be deducted but if the umpire judges that either or both batsmen have deliberately run short then he can, after the ball is no longer in play, disallow any runs completed and ask the batsmen to return to their original ends.

● THE SCORERS

The Laws require that scorers are appointed to ensure the totals are accurately recorded and the match result is thereby established without dispute. As the best game is one diligently controlled by capable umpires, so a match faithfully and clearly recorded by knowledgeable scorers is perfectly summarized and officially documented. In the unfortunate circumstances where inadequate record is kept of the game the resulting errors and inaccuracies can only cause problems and perhaps mar an otherwise happy contest.

The scorer who takes the task seriously will, like an umpire, be prepared for all eventualities. Personal equipment will include:

- pencils and a sharpener or fine-point ball pens
- watch
- a copy of this book or the official MCC Laws of Cricket

- a copy of any specific rules under which the match is being played
- notepaper in case a message has to be sent to the umpires.

The scorer should also be aware of the following matters *before* the start of play:

- the hours of play and the timing and duration of the intervals
- whether six- or eight-ball overs are to be bowled
- the time at which the last hour of play will start and how it will be signalled
- the location, method of operation and manning of the scoreboard
- any local agreement relating to boundary markings and allowances
- what clock or watch will be used for match timings.

Though some of these actions appear to duplicate the role of the umpires this only serves to demonstrate that the two pairs of officials should act in partnership. With this in mind, scorers should also know of any limitation on overs which may be bowled in an innings or by each bowler even though this is formally the responsibility of the umpires.

Inaccurate scoring causes problems but can be avoided if the scorers:

- refer to the laws of the game if uncertain of the action they should take
- query any unclear signals from the umpires at the time they arise and request precise signalling

- regularly check with the opponents' scorer and scorebook
- ensure the scoreboard is regularly updated to match their records.

Scorers must know and be able to recognize umpiring signals, especially to distinguish between those which are similar. They must acknowledge these signals immediately and clearly and should never assume they have missed a signal or that an umpire has failed to give one. For example, the scorer may often believe a leg bye has been scored because he is too far away to have detected that the ball did hit the bat and that the runs should be credited to the batsman. Unless the leg bye is signalled any run taken must be regarded as a score to the batsman on strike. Even if a scorer is certain the umpire has made a wrong decision he must react to, and record, any given signal. If the signal given is unclear or the reasons for it not understood, then the scorer must ask for clarification.

If a fielder indicates that a catch has been taken clearly or a boundary scored, the scorer must still await the signal from the umpire.

If the umpire allows too few or too many balls in an over the scorer should record that number and only raise the matter if it persists or the umpires seek confirmation of the number of balls remaining.

● THE SCOREBOOK

Although there are various styles of scorebook design available, the constituent parts are the same. Regular scorers will come to favour a layout which they are comfortable with.

The sections of a scorebook are as follows:

- **The batting order**. The scorer should obtain this from the captain of the batting side and request that he be advised of any alteration. The scorer is well advised to keep the list to one side and only enter the names in the book when the order is confirmed as the game progresses
- **Record of the batsman's score**. All runs scored off the bat are recorded here
- **How out**. The method of dismissal is indicated here. If a substitute fielder makes the catch the wicket is shown as 'Caught sub'; if a striker is dismissed by the wicketkeeper because his runner is out of his ground the book should show 'Run Out'; if a batsman touches the ball with his bat but the ball still breaks the wicket, he is out 'Bowled'; if the wicketkeeper breaks the stumps with the ball in his gloves or by the ball rebounding from his body the batsman is 'Stumped' unless the umpire considers he was attempting

a run, in which case the decision will be 'Run Out'. Where doubt exists the scorer should leave the space vacant and obtain clarification as soon as possible

- **Running total**. Most commonly numbers are struck off a consecutive list as each run is scored
- **Record of all extras** scored or awarded (byes, wides, leg byes, etc.)
- **The fall of wickets**. The lower line records the number in the batting order of the player dismissed
- **The bowlers' names** listed in the order they commence bowling
- **Record of extras** which are added to the bowler's analysis, such as wides and no-balls
- **Bowling analysis summary**.

The amount of detail shown in a scorebook depends on the professionalism of the scorer and the needs of the club concerned. In addition to the major statistics of the

A typical scorebook. This charts a typical innings; the following common incidents are recorded in the bowlers' analysis:

a – Four byes scored off fifth ball but still a maiden

b – No ball. The striker did not hit the ball but two runs were taken. Extra ball allowed

c – Wide ball. No runs scored

d – Single scored, then four overthrows. Five runs to the striker; batsmen have changed ends

e – No ball. No runs scored. Extra ball allowed

f – Run out. Not credited to the bowler.

Batting

#	BATSMEN	RUNS SCORED	HOW OUT	BOWLER	TOTAL
1	B. AMES	1.2.1.1.1.1.	st. GREEN	NUNN	8
2	C. BELL	1.2.4.2.1.4	HIT WICKET	LOWE	16
3	D. COLE	4.4.4.2.	ct BROWN	MEAD	14
4	E. DALE	5.2.4.2.2.3.4.1.2.4.	RUN OUT	OUT	31
5	F. ELMS		ct & bowled	NUNN	0
6	G. FELL	2.4.2.1.2.1.2.1.1.	NOT OUT	OUT	16
7	H. GILL	2.1.4.4.3.6.	ct BLACK	NUNN	20
8	I. HALL	2.1.	BOWLED	OWEN	3
9	J. IKIN	4.	LBW	OWEN	4
10	K. JUDD	2.2.4.1.4.4.	BOWLED	NUNN	17
11	L. KEMP		ct GREEN	MEAD	0

BYES 4
LEG BYES 1
WIDES
NO BALLS 3

TOTAL RUNS 129
TOTAL EXTRAS 8
TOTAL 137 FOR 10 WKTS.

Runs at the fall of each wicket and No. of outgoing batsman

1	2	3	4	5	6	7	8	9	10
23	42	68	76	76	96	99	109	130	137
2	3	1	4	5	7	8	6	10	11

Bowling Analysis

#	BOWLERS	OVERS	M'DNS	RUNS	WKTS	AV'GE
1	M. LOWE	8	1	37	1	37.00
2	N. MEAD	8.5	0	33	2	16.50
3	O. NUNN	8	1	33	4	8.25
4	P. OWEN	5	0	30	2	15.00

match, a scorebook can be transformed into a diverse summary of the game which, with close examination, can give a very full understanding of the pattern of the game months or even years after the event.

Some scorers use different colours to denote bowlers and batsmen or add every possible detail about playing conditions, timing of innings, etc. However, a scorer's first aim is to provide an indisputable record of the game as it was played. The scorebook may be used many weeks after the game, for example, to compile club averages. It will also be filed in club archives.

● THE RESULT

The result of a match is a win either by runs for the team batting first or by wickets still to fall for the team batting second.

A tie occurs only when the scores are equal at the cessation of play. To ensure a winner, some rules under which the game has been played may award a tied game to the team losing fewer wickets.

BATTING

● EQUIPMENT

We dealt with the shape and design of the cricket bat in the chapter on 'The Bat and the Ball' earlier. Batsmen will normally also be equipped with gloves, pads and abdominal protector; these and other items such as helmets and thigh pads are not covered by the Laws of cricket.

● SUBSTITUTES AND RUNNERS

Only the eleven players nominated at the start of play are allowed to bat. If one of the team is unable to bat, a substitute is not allowed, though an injured batsman is allowed a runner (Law 2).

A runner should wear the same external equipment as the injured batsman and, wherever possible, have already batted in the innings. The positions taken by a runner are shown in the chart overleaf.

A batsman who has accepted the services of a runner remains subject to the laws of the game and can be dismissed in the usual ways. His runner can be given out, and the batsman with him, through obstructing the field, handling the ball and being run out. He can also be given run out or stumped if the wicket at the striker's end is broken while he is out of his ground.

● DISMISSALS

A batsman cannot be given out by the umpire unless an appeal is made *to* the umpire by the fielding side. In practice,

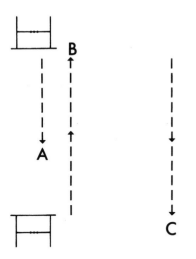

A Injured batsman on strike

B Non-striker

C Runner

Positions taken when a batsman has a runner.

Injured batsman hits the ball and his two team mates take a single

of course, many dismissals do not require an appeal to have them accepted by the parties involved. The various ways of getting out are discussed below.

Bowled

A batsman is out bowled if the ball, delivered by the bowler, breaks his wicket by dislodging one or both bails. This is the case even if the ball touches the bat or the batsman's body, bounces more than once or hits the wicket on the full. The dismissal is also termed 'bowled' if the ball strikes his pads in a position which would result in his being given out 'leg before wicket' but then deflects onto the wicket and breaks it.

There is seldom any dispute when a batsman is bowled; the evidence is plain for all to see. There can be some doubt in circumstances where a strong wind may dislodge a bail as a ball is delivered or where a wicketkeeper is standing close to the wicket and accidentally removes a bail when moving in his stance. In both cases the umpire at the batsman's end may be in a better position to see and can be consulted before a decision is made.

A batsman will not be given out bowled if he hits, or kicks the ball onto, his wicket *after* fully completing a stroke; for example, in attempting to regain his ground to avoid being run out or stumped. In such circumstances the umpire will need to judge whether the stroke has been fully completed.

Caught

The batsman is out caught if the ball strikes the bat, or the hand or glove which is holding the bat, and is caught by a fielder before it touches the ground.

A **catch** is valid if:

- the fielder stays within the field of play until he has control of the ball (see the first chapter, on 'The Ground and the Pitch')
- the ball is clutched against the body or accidentally lodges in the clothing of the catcher or the wicketkeeper's pads
- the ball does not touch the ground even if the hand holding the ball does
- the ball strikes an umpire, another fielder or either batsman before being otherwise lawfully caught
- the ball is caught off an obstruction within the field of play provided it has not been previously agreed that the obstacle is to be considered a boundary marker.

What makes a fair catch?

Fair catch

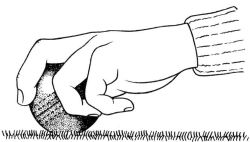

Not out

A catch is not valid if the ball first hits, or lodges in, a protective helmet being worn by a fielder.

Deciding on a caught dismissal can be very straightforward or one of the toughest umpiring judgements. The latter can include catches to the wicketkeeper when the ball may only faintly graze the bat or glove, when a ball is edged into the pads before being caught or where the catcher's hand and the ball are very close to the ground. In the latter case the umpire at the bowler's end may choose to consult the other umpire if he may have had a better view.

Umpires and players will become accustomed to distinguishing between the sounds of the ball hitting pad, bat and clothing but everyone can still be misled if the ball passes the bat as the latter flicks the ground or the pad. The efficient umpire will seldom rely on sounds alone and will train himself to watch for deviation in flight and the close-quarter deflections which can decide 'close calls'.

A catch can be taken off bat, gloves or wrist.

Against short-pitched bowling in particular a ball may be 'caught' by a wicketkeeper or close fielder after hitting part of the batsman other than the bat, hand or wrist. If a batsman takes evasive action or plays a hook shot at the ball and at the same time he is hit on the shoulder, forearm or chest, this is not out. He is also not out if the ball strikes a hand which is not holding the bat.

If the ball lodges in the clothing of the striker, either umpire or the helmet of any player, the bowler's umpire will call 'Dead Ball'.

Leg before wicket

This method of dismissal will always create most controversy because, particularly in the amateur game, umpires may be unsure of the law and how to interpret it, especially in the heat of the moment.

Law 36 is short and clear. A batsman is out **leg before wicket** (LBW) if, in attempting to play a stroke, a ball which would have hit the wicket strikes any part of his body, clothing or equipment before it has touched his bat or a hand holding it, provided that the ball has pitched on a straight line between the wickets, on the **off side** of the striker's wicket. If the ball strikes the batsman on the full, then if the point of impact is in a straight line between the sets of stumps, it is given out. This decision is also given if the ball strikes the batsman on the pads, body or equipment other than his bat

(helmet, thigh pad) outside the line of the off stump if the umpire judges that he had not played a shot, and that the ball would have broken the wicket.

The diagrams on pp. 46 and 48–9 put you in the umpiring position at the bowler's end and also a side-on location. To make the illustration clear the bat is not close to the line of the ball. In a match this is not often the case – the umpire's first decision is often whether the ball has touched the bat or not.

With every ball bowled, the umpire should follow this sequence of checks – just in case an LBW appeal is made. He should watch for the direction (angle) of delivery, movement in the air, the change of angle (if any) after pitching, the degree of lift from the bounce and the likelihood of it hitting the stumps if not intercepted. This process demands a series of questions, asked and answered in a moment.

- did the ball hit the pad on the full, or pitch outside off stump or in line with the stumps, wicket to wicket?
- did the ball hit the batsman or his equipment and not the bat, or the hand holding it, before doing so?
- was the point of impact in line, wicket to wicket, even if it was above the height of the bails?
- would the ball have hit the wicket?

In the event of the batsman not attempting a stroke the same questions are applicable but the third question can allow the point of impact to be outside the line of the off stump.

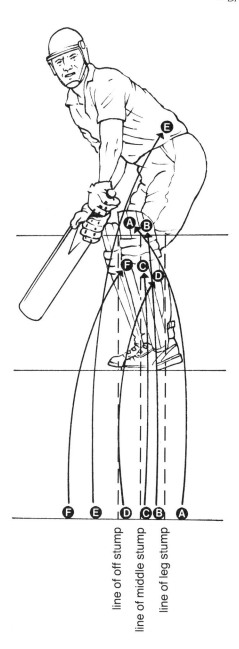

Leg before wicket

a – is not out as the ball has pitched outside leg stump

b – is probably not out as it has hit the pad above the height of the stumps

c – out

d – is probably not out as the line of the ball suggests it will miss leg stump. It is certainly not out if the batsman is well forward from his wicket

e – not out, as the ball will pass over the stumps

f – out if the ball is not going to miss leg stump. Provided the pad is in line with the stumps when the ball hits, it does not matter that the ball has pitched outside the off stump, as the batsman is not offering a stroke.

line of off stump

line of middle stump

line of leg stump

Opposite Out! The umpire has answered in the affirmative the split-second questions which arise at an LBW appeal and gives his decision.

• Only if all of these questions can be answered 'yes' can the umpire raise his index finger and give the batsman out.

The most common reason for not giving an LBW decision is a negative answer to the last question above. The umpire must be certain that the ball would have hit the wicket; if he has *any* doubt the decision has to be not out. If the ball has been regularly bouncing above stump height or bowlers have been achieving lateral movement (swing, spin, cut) then the point of impact has to be very close to the stumps for the umpire to be sure the

The umpire has to make a split-second decision – has the ball hit the bat or the pad – or both, and if both, in what order.

ball would have hit them; strokes attempted on the front foot, that is, where the batsman is a long way from the wicket when the ball makes its impact, are a common cause of the appeal being rejected.

If, in the flourish of the attempted stroke, the umpire cannot be sure that the ball did not touch the bat first then he must also give a 'not out' response, in the same way that he will if the ball pitches outside the line of the leg stump before hitting the batsman.

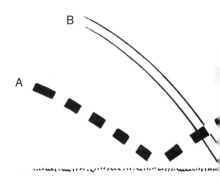

Umpires, and players who may have to undertake that role, are well advised to 'stand' during net sessions to become even more acquainted with the task of answering leg before wicket appeals. They may even choose to bowl at a vacant wicket themselves to see how many times they think the ball is going to hit the stumps but still passes wide of them.

The decisions given for LBW must be as impartial as any other, and a clear law is provided, but umpires

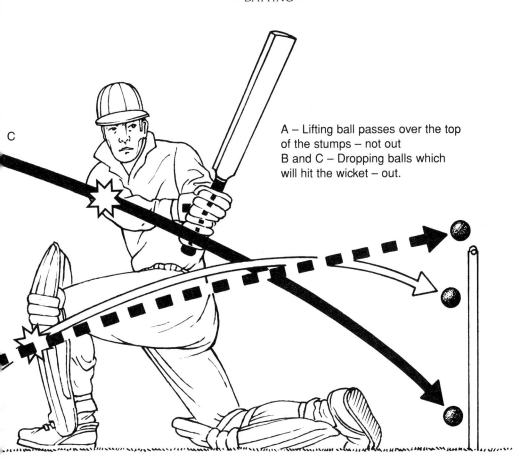

C

A – Lifting ball passes over the top of the stumps – not out
B and C – Dropping balls which will hit the wicket – out.

should guard against both giving a batsman 'out' simply because he has not played a stroke – the four questions still have to be answered in the affirmative – and giving in to an appeal because of the number he has already rejected. A batsman cannot be given out because of the ignorance of the rules by those playing against him!

Various myths cloud the leg before wicket dismissal. For example, while angle of delivery is a major factor to consider, it should never be said that a particular form of bowling, such as round the wicket or from wide of the crease, cannot produce a positive decision. Similarly, an LBW appeal from a full toss is sometimes rejected for the very reason that the delivery was of that style when, actually, the umpire may have a clearer view of its line to the stumps because it has not bounced and deviated. The only factors to consider are those summarized by the questions above, whatever the style of bowling.

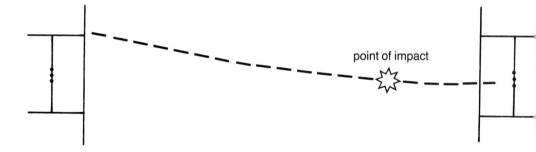

point of impact

A ball bowled from wide of the crease or from around the wicket can still secure an LBW decision if the umpire sees the line of the ball straighten through the air or off the pitch.

Hit wicket

The batsman is out **hit wicket** if his stumps are broken by his bat, his body, or any part of his clothing or equipment while he is preparing to receive or is receiving or playing a delivery or is beginning his first run immediately after playing, or attempting to play, the ball or if he breaks his wicket in this manner while making a second stroke to guard his wicket within the provisions of Law 34.1.

This dismissal can, in other words, be caused by the bat striking the stumps in its backlift during playing the stroke; by the feet sliding back in the crease; the tip of the pad dislodging a bail; or the batsman hitting the stumps in his follow-through. Less common is for a cap or helmet to fall onto the wicket during the stroke.

A batsman is *not* dismissed hit wicket if the wicket is broken while he is running for other than his first run or avoiding a throw-in.

The decision often requires consultation between the umpires to ensure there can have been no other reason for the wicket being broken. It is relatively rare for batsmen to be dismissed in this way.

Stumped

If a batsman leaves his crease during the delivery of the ball and the wicketkeeper breaks the wicket with the ball in his hands or by it rebounding from his body, then the striker is out **stumped**. To effect a fair dismissal the ball must hit the wicket or be held by a glove which does so; the wicketkeeper must wait for the ball to pass behind the wicket, unless it has touched the batsman.

The batsman is stumped rather than run out if the wicket is broken before a run is attempted. This dismissal is usually accomplished in a split second and at great pace, and is judged by the umpire at the striker's end, standing at square leg or point.

Stumped. If the wicketkeeper breaks the
wicket, he must have the ball in his gloves.
The batsman must have part of his foot or the
bat in his hand touching the ground behind
the popping crease to avoid dismissal. He is
out of his ground if his foot or bat are behind
the crease but off the ground.

Stumped. In the top example, even though the heel is behind the line it is not grounded – out. In the second illustration, the foot is grounded behind the back of the crease – not out.

Pages 52 and 53 In? The camera never lies and the bail appears to be dislodged while David Gower's foot is still off the ground. He was given 'not out' but the umpire did not have the advantage of this photograph.

The umpire must watch for whether the foot or the bat held in the hand is grounded *behind* the popping crease at the moment the bail is dislodged. If the batsman's raised heel is behind the crease but off the ground, or his bat is beyond the crease but in the air, then he is out of his ground; the back of the crease line denotes the batsman's ground; on the line is out. If he is content that the batsman is out of his ground he must then be certain the wicketkeeper has control of the ball in his gloves when the wicket is broken or that the ball rebounding from the wicketkeeper is responsible for removing the bails.

The wicket can often be broken by the wicketkeeper's gloves without the ball being firmly held by them or by his pads brushing against the stumps as he moves for the ball. The umpire at the striker's end will need extra concentration whenever the wicketkeeper takes a position close to the stumps. If he has any doubt the decision must be not out.

The wicketkeeper must wait for the ball to pass the stumps before he takes it and he must be holding it when his gloves break the wicket.

Run out

Either batsman can be dismissed **run out** if, at any time while the ball is in play other than the circumstances for which he can be given out stumped, he is out of his ground and the wicket is broken. If the batsmen pass each other (**cross**) while attempting a run, the player running to the wicket which is broken is dismissed even if he did not play the most recent stroke; if they have not crossed then the player who has left the broken wicket is given out even if he is the non-striker. The illustrations on pp. 58–9 indicate which batsman is given out depending on their position at the breaking of the wicket.

The striker receiving a no-ball cannot be run out unless he attempts a run; a batsman leaving his crease to avoid injury cannot be run out in any circumstances.

Only the run being attempted at the time of the run out is not scored; those already completed from the same stroke are counted. A batsman making use of a runner because of injury is dismissed if his runner fails to make his ground while attempting a run on the injured player's behalf; the injured batsman can record no runs from a stroke if his runner is dismissed in this manner.

The run out dismissal is not allowed if the ball breaks the opposite wicket without first touching a fielder.

While a bowler gets the credit for a stumping he does not do so for a run out.

In the drama of a run out the umpires will be chiefly concerned with whether the batsman makes his ground and that, to whichever end the ball is thrown, the wicket is broken correctly. The ball must be in the hand which breaks the wicket, if it does not hit the stumps directly.

Timed out

A batsman will be given **timed out** if he wilfully takes more than two minutes to reach the field of play from the moment of the fall of the previous wicket. An appeal has to be made and the umpire has to be satisfied that unfair advantage is being deliberately sought by the batting team by time-wasting.

This rule (Law 31) seeks to avoid time-wasting, particularly when the time lost may negatively affect the chances of the fielding side. Umpires will need to use their discretion as to whether the law should be enforced but, if an appeal is made, they are duty bound to consider it and make an adjudication.

Time lost in this manner should be added to the normal close of play.

Handled the ball

Though a rare form of dismissal there have been examples of leading professional cricketers being given out **handled the ball**. Law 33 states that a batsman will be given out if he touches a ball in play with his free hand. The law includes the word 'wilfully', indicating that the player

Run out.

This batsman is in if his bat is touching the ground.

You can dive to attempt to make your ground, but the bat must be grounded over the popping crease while in your hand.

This batsman is run out.

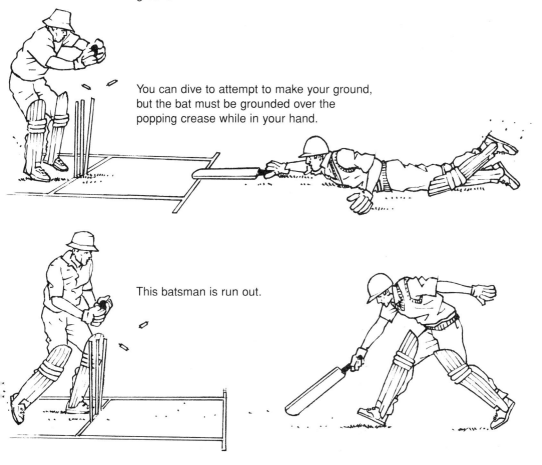

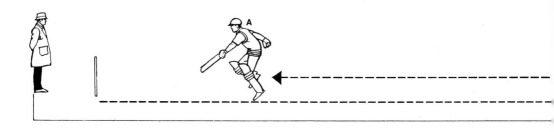

In the top example batsman B is out because the two players have crossed. In the second illustration it is batsman A who is out because they have not crossed.

should not be seeking advantage in protecting his wicket, preventing a catch or scoring runs. The umpire will judge whether such action has had this result.

The law also states that the batsman may touch the ball 'with the consent' of the opposition; therefore the courtesy of picking up a 'dead ball' for a fielder should usually be accompanied by a glance to confirm that the fielding side consider the action acceptable.

The most common reason for this mode of dismissal is where the

batsman reacts without thinking to the sight of the ball falling from his body towards the stumps. Though he can deflect the ball with his foot or bat, without then attempting a run, this law prohibits the use of the hand not holding the bat to protect the wicket. The bowler does not get credit for these dismissals.

Hit the ball twice

Law 34 states that, if the fielding side appeal, a batsman must be given out if he 'uses his bat or his person' to return the ball to any of the fielding side. This may sound severe but it is a law which the umpires are duty bound to employ. The fundamental reason for this ruling is to prevent more than one stroke being made; there can be few players who are not aware of the illegality of taking two hits. It is

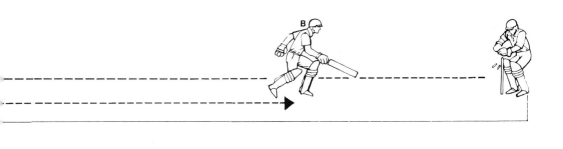

possible for a player to react quickly to a ball which hits his body and he is in a position to hit it with the bat. The umpire must see that such action is wilful rather than defensive and aimed at gaining an advantage if he is to give the batsman out.

Obstructing the field
If the umpire decides that a batsman has wilfully obstructed the opposition by word or deed, he shall, on appeal, dismiss the player for **obstructing the field**. The bowler does not get credit for the wicket.

This very rare form of dismissal might occur when a batsman, striker or non-striker, deliberately calls out to confuse or distract a fielder attempting a catch or physically obstructs or baulks a player moving for a catch, attempting to stop the ball or trying

for a run out. A batsman can also be dismissed in this manner if he prevents a wicketkeeper or fielder from taking a catch even if he is genuinely playing a second stroke to protect his wicket.

Out from a No-Ball
A batsman can be out from a **no-ball** if he contravenes Law 34, and he and the non-striker can be **run out** or dismissed for **handling the ball** or **obstructing the field**.

BOWLING

The bowler is the spearhead of a team's efforts to dismiss their opponents. He must keep at the forefront of his mind the state of the game, the strategic plan of his team, his own scheme for dismissing each batsman and for containing their run scoring, and the various field placings he needs to maximize his success. He should also be aware of the laws constraining his behaviour on the field.

Bowlers, and their fielding colleagues, are guilty of unfair play (Law 42) if they 'lift' the seam of the ball or alter the ball's condition in any other way by 'unnatural' means including abrasives, tools, fingernails and creams.

The bowling of fast short-pitched balls and high full tosses is also controlled by Law 42 and is a controversial subject at all levels of the game. Rules introduced for specific international or professional competitions may be additional to the

basic law which is perfectly clear for routine games, leaving umpires to be the sole arbiter in enforcing the rule.

According to Law 42, a short-pitched ball is unfair if it is considered to be an attempt to intimidate the batsman and, by its length, height or direction, appears to be intended or likely to cause physical injury. The umpire is required to also take into consideration the skill of the batsman to defend himself. The umpire can take action, from the first example of such a delivery should he so wish, by calling a no-ball, cautioning the bowler and advising his captain, the batsman and his fellow umpire of his action. When a second similar delivery is bowled the same procedure is followed and a final warning is given to the bowler.

These warnings stay in force if the bowler changes end or returns to bowl a second spell. If he contravenes the law again the umpire will direct the captain of the fielding side to take the bowler off and complete the over with

A fast, high, full-pitched delivery which passes the batsman above waist height must be called a no-ball.

another player. The offending player cannot bowl again in that innings. The umpire may also choose to report the incident to the officials of both clubs and the governing body for the match.

The same action is taken for fast, high full-pitched deliveries, which have recently been redefined as ones which pass without bouncing above waist height of a batsman standing upright in the crease.

The bowler delivers six or eight balls to complete an over, the number depending on the rules of the game concerned. He can change ends as often as he wishes but cannot bowl two overs consecutively. If a bowler is unable to complete an over because of illness, injury or suspension another member of the fielding side, other than the player due to deliver the next over, must complete the number of remaining balls.

If an over is left unfinished at an interval or at other interruption to play, it must be completed when play is resumed. Where the umpire has miscounted but still called 'Over', the over stands, even if the umpire realizes his error, or has it drawn to his attention later. The ball is 'dead' immediately upon 'Over' being called.

Devon Malcolm's front foot is clearly behind the popping crease for this delivery.

Finally, the bowler must guard against contravening the few regulations which exist for field placing. He must have no more than two fielders behind the popping crease on the leg side and not allow fielders to stand or lean across the pitch – 10 ft (3.05 m) in width – while the ball is in play.

● THE DELIVERY AND FOLLOW-THROUGH

The bowler must advise the umpire standing at his end of the action he will use, that is, which arm he bowls with, and what side (over or around the wicket) he will bowl from, so that the batsman can also be notified. Failure to do this, or to change an action without such notification, is deemed to be unfair play and the umpire should call a no-ball.

For a delivery to be acceptable the bowler's back foot must land within the inner edge of the return crease or its extension and some part of the front foot must remain behind the back edge of the popping crease before the ball is delivered. Also, the bowling arm must be straight during the delivery swing; in other words, the ball must be fairly 'bowled' and not thrown. The umpire at the bowler's end will call a no ball if the feet are not correctly placed but his colleague at the striker's end will usually be better placed to adjudicate on an incorrect arm action.

A no ball is judged, and called, at the moment of delivery; a **wide ball** is assessed as it passes the striker. Some competitions, especially those based on a limited number of overs, may have extra rules for what will constitute a wide delivery. In most types of cricket it is classed as a ball which passes out of reach of the batsman, above or to the side, when he is standing in his normal guard position. A ball cannot be called wide if a batsman moves towards the line of the ball, making it reachable, or if he moves away from the line of the ball. Should a wide ball be called early and the striker then reaches the delivery, the call is revoked. If the batsman is caught after hitting a wide ball the dismissal stands, as do the decisions stumped, hit wicket, and run out if the batsman is attempting a run.

After delivery of the ball the bowler must run off the pitch to avoid damaging the playing surface. The umpire must ensure this practice is followed and will pay particular attention to an area two feet wide running from four feet in front of each popping crease where most balls pitch on a 'good length'. The umpire should warn any bowler who, in his normal follow-through, runs into this protected area. If the bowler persists, the umpire should issue one final warning and then prohibit him from bowling for the rest of the innings.

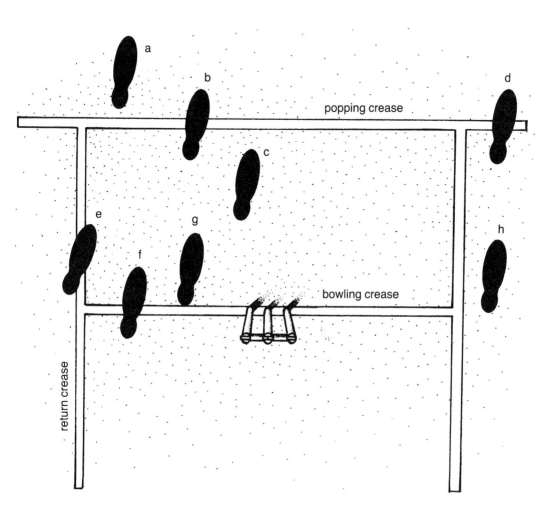

No-ball
* a, b, c and d represent the front foot
* b, c and d are legal
* a is a no-ball
* e, f, g and h represent the back foot
* e and h are no-balls
* f and g are legal provided the corresponding front foot is legal.

The crease markings play no part in the calling of a wide save for their being a guide to the measuring process the umpire may use to make his decision.

The arm must remain straight throughout the arc of delivery.

Bowlers must not run into the
shaded area in their
follow-through.

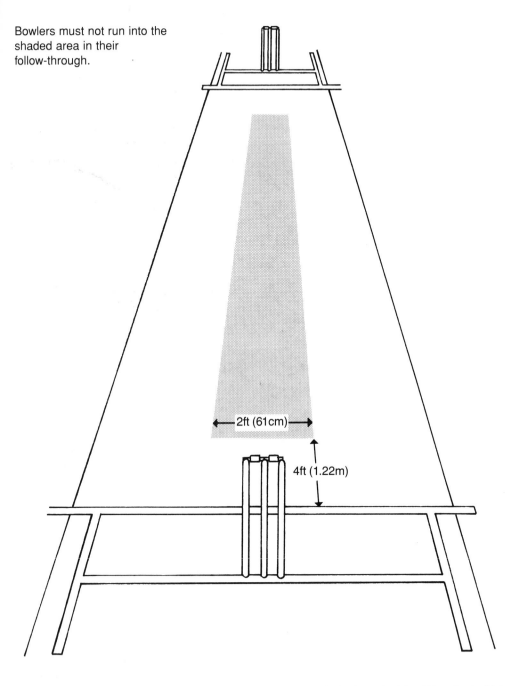

2ft (61cm)

4ft (1.22m)

Overleaf A close decision! Has the ball hit
the bat or merely the pad?

● APPEALS

Though many dismissals cause no dispute and do not require an appeal for the batsman to accept that he is out, the bowler should be aware that according to Law 27 an umpire cannot give a batsman out unless the bowler, or a team-mate, appeals before the next delivery is begun by the bowler commencing his run up.

The appeal, **'How's That?'**, should be directed at the umpire at the bowler's end except for those claiming dismissals by hit wicket, stumped or run out, which may well involve the official at the striker's end.

Remember that it is possible for a first appeal to be rejected and a second accepted by the same or the other umpire. A bowler may appeal for a leg before wicket decision but, if the appeal is disallowed, may be able to claim a bat/pad catch. Similarly, a claim for a catch by a wicketkeeper may be rejected by the umpire at the bowler's end only for the wicketkeeper to react quickly enough to remove the bails with the ball in his glove and appeal for a stumping dismissal from the umpire at his end.

An umpire may choose not to call a wide ball if the batsman moves from his stance towards or away from the path of the ball.

Opposite The bowler must run away from the centre of the pitch in his follow-through.

Overleaf A catch cannot be taken if a ball rebounds from a fielder's helmet but a ball deflecting from another part of his body can be caught and the batsman dismissed.

FIELDING

● STOPPING THE BALL

The fielder may not stop the ball with his cap, helmet or sweater and if he does so, five runs are immediately awarded and added to any runs already completed. If a ball strikes such an item on the ground, or thrown at it, the same penalty runs are scored.

● FIELDING POSITIONS

No more than two fielders may be behind the popping crease on the leg side and no member of the fielding side may stand on the pitch while the ball is in play and until the ball has passed the batsman or been played by him. The wicketkeeper must remain behind the wicket until the ball has passed the batsman or been hit by him.

● SUBSTITUTE FIELDERS

Fielders injured or becoming ill during the course of the game will normally be allowed to be substituted. The umpires may allow substitutes in other exceptional circumstances but should seek the agreement of the opposing captain. Substitutes are not allowed to bowl or keep wicket, although a player returning after substitution may play any role but only after he has been on the field for the same period of time that he was substituted.

Should the umpire believe a player has begun the game with an injury he may use his discretionary powers to disallow a substitution.

● FIELD POSITIONS

Though the positions taken by players are not part of the rules of the game, it is important that all cricketers become aware of the names and locations. Apart from other benefits this avoids delay and encourages efficient captaincy. For these reasons we provide the chart on p. 78:

Illegal fielding positions.
1. Only two fielders are allowed behind the crease on the legside. Fielders A or B must move as shown.
2. Fielders must not stand on the pitch as the ball is bowled. Fielder D must ensure he does not encroach onto the shaded area.

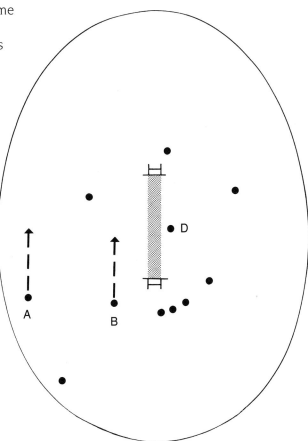

Overleaf Provided the fielder has control of the ball and prevents it from touching the ground, the catch is fair – even if the hand holding the ball hits the ground.

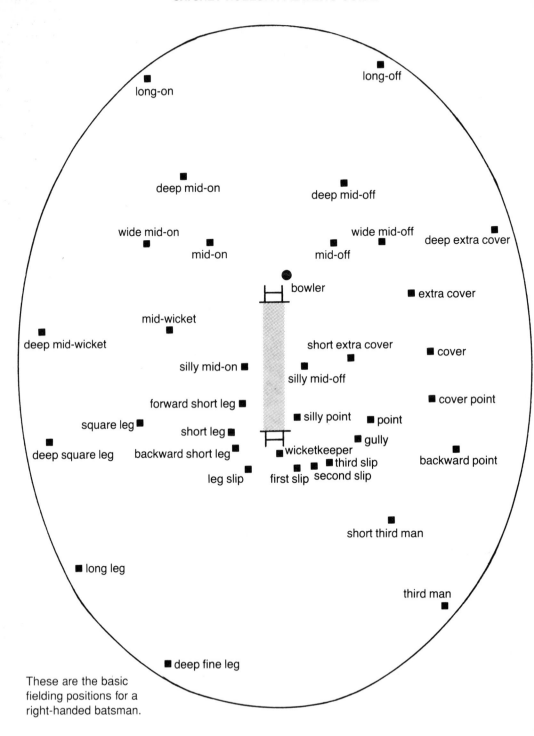

long-off

long-on

deep mid-on

deep mid-off

wide mid-on

wide mid-off

deep extra cover

mid-on

mid-off

bowler

extra cover

mid-wicket

deep mid-wicket

short extra cover

cover

silly mid-on

silly mid-off

forward short leg

cover point

square leg

silly point

point

short leg

gully

deep square leg

backward short leg

wicketkeeper

backward point

leg slip

first slip

third slip

second slip

short third man

long leg

third man

deep fine leg

These are the basic
fielding positions for a
right-handed batsman.

INDEX